RAISING
BOYS INTO
EXTRAORDINARY
YOUNG MEN

A Mother's Perspective

Monica Hawkins, Ph.D., M.P.H.

authorHOUSE®

AuthorHouse™
1663 Liberty Drive
Bloomington, IN 47403
www.authorhouse.com
Phone: 1 (800) 839-8640

Published by AuthorHouse 05/13/2018

ISBN: 978-1-5462-2960-5 (sc)
ISBN: 978-1-5462-2959-9 (e)

This book is dedicated to our extraordinary son Therman Hawkins III, his future children, and his future grandchildren.

Preface

This book will change you and your son's lives. It is written for every baby boy who is born so that he will grow up to be one of society's successful and extraordinary young men. As the mother of an extraordinary, self-confident, and intelligent young man, I know that there will be many obstacles that you and your sons will face throughout life. Society sometimes struggles with accepting extraordinary boys being successful, but it is my life's mission that your sons will become successful anyway. I want your sons to always exude self-confidence, mental-strength, intelligence, and other similar characteristics in every situation they encounter. I want the same characteristics to be developed in your sons as my son so that they, too, can always stand out in a group setting. I want them to always be noticeable in a group setting in positive ways. This means that they need to be assertive in every situation they face so that people will always recognize them. I know that this is easier said than done and that they may get extremely nervous speaking up all the time, and that is totally understandable. The more that your sons practice being assertive, they will soon begin to feel more comfortable each time displaying self-confidence. As an extraordinary parent, your job is to always create a safe place for your sons to be raised. This environment should include giving them basic needs such as food, water, shelter, and tender love and care. Spend time displaying love and affection toward your sons. You owe it to them so that they can then display love and affection toward their own children when they get older.

I want to pass along my blueprint that I used to raise my son to be a mentally-strong, articulate, intelligent, extraordinary young man who was taught each of these characteristics from the moment he was born. I am a true believer that you are what you think. So, if your sons believe that they are extraordinary, then they will be extraordinary. From the time my son was a baby, people from all cultural backgrounds would ask me what I was doing special with him because he was so intelligent, alert, and curious. After my son learned to talk, he would hold a conversation with anyone that he wanted to talk with and who would talk with him. Most people enjoyed talking with him. He was an extremely calm baby and his demeanor was the same every day. He was also a very engaging and alert baby. He did not cry a lot and whenever he did it was usually because he was hungry or sleepy. My son never needed a pacifier as a baby to be soothed, which is extremely unusual. I always sang to him whenever he was fussy or needed to eat or drink. I did not necessarily have a beautiful voice, but I had a voice that my son always recognized and would almost instantaneously calm him down. My son started going to a day care center when he was about two years old that was very close to my home. It was important that he was close to our home so that we could spend as much time with him as possible. At the day care center, my son was well-loved by all his teachers because he always had such a positive attitude. His day care center teachers always told me that since my son's attitude was happy every day they rarely filled in his daily behavior form each day. At first, I thought that my son's teachers did not want to fill in his daily behavior form because they were too busy. I quickly realized that they would be filling in the same information every day. Whenever prospective couples or individuals toured my son's day care center, they would always notice him. If they returned to visit they would always look for my son. If he was in another room taking a nap and they did not see him they would always ask "where is that baby that is always so energetic and curious that we saw the other day?"

To this day my son always stands out from other young boys because of his leadership skills and great character. I want the same for your sons too. You, too, can raise intelligent, self-confident, and extraordinary young men and leaders. "Train up a child in the way he should go, and when he is old he will not depart from it (Proverbs 22:6).

Table of Contents

CHAPTER 1

MY VISION FOR MY EXTRAORDINARY BABY

Before I was pregnant with my son I knew that I would be an extremely involved mother. I had a vision in mind for him from the moment I knew that I was pregnant. I knew that my son would be extremely intelligent and extraordinary and that my husband and I would always want the best for him. A support system for babies at an early age is extremely important for them. Before my son was born I knew I would take an extended amount of time off from my job. This allowed me to spend as much time as possible with my son during the initial stages of his life. It was extremely important that whenever my son would wake up that he constantly would see his mom's face filled with tender love and care. Staying at home with my son, when he was a baby, was some of the best times of my life. I wanted to be around my son so that I could see his first everything. His first smile, roll over, coo, and sip from a sippy cup. While my son was a baby, I spent a lot of quality time with him. I spent an enormous amount of time walking around the neighborhood with him. This was good for both of us. It was good for me because it gave me an opportunity to shed those excess pounds that I had gained during my pregnancy. It was good for my son because he was able to see the beautiful world that surrounded him.

My son was exposed to all types of soothing and relaxing music since he was inside my womb. As a baby, he always enjoyed listening to classical music. Every night, before my son went to sleep, I would turn on classical music on the radio on his nightstand. I started this routine when he was a baby. As a toddler my son quickly grew to love listening to classical music so much that whenever I forgot to turn on the music, he quickly got out of his bed and let me know that I forgot to turn on his music. When this first happened, I was elated because it meant that he loved listening to classical music as he fell asleep every night. I know the music soothed him. To this day, my son still enjoys listening to classical music whenever he goes to sleep at night.

Our closeness to this day first began with our closeness when my son was a baby. It is one of the reasons that my son has always been so self-confident and extraordinary. My son knows that my husband and I will always be there for him no matter what situations that he will face in life. Another vision that I had before I was pregnant with my son was that I was going to breastfeed him. One of the reasons that I always wanted to breastfeed him was because I was certain that it would help his immune system to be strong.[1] My son had a strong immune system that was built early on from him being breastfed. He rarely got sick as a baby.

CHAPTER 2

BE READY FOR YOUR SON'S BIRTH

Address any problems that will possibly affect you being a great parent raising your boys into extraordinary young men and leaders. If prospective parents are stressed in their lives, then it may not be the best time to have a child. Consider waiting until you are not real stressed out. Having a child is the most unselfish thing that a woman can do. Once women have children they must always prioritize and put their child's needs and wants before their own. This sometimes means not buying or waiting a little longer to buy some of the items that you want to instantly buy. A lot of women forget this and put themselves first. Once a woman is pregnant with a child she must remember that life is no longer about her but about your child. Selfish parents will usually produce a selfish son. Train your sons not to be selfish. If you do not train them to be unselfish then they will grow up to be users and takers instead of givers. Your sons deserve the best life that their soon-to-be parents can give them. When a woman is pregnant consider reading to your unborn son. Your unborn son will constantly hear his mother's voice, which can relax and calm him while inside the womb. Also, sing to your sons when you are pregnant. A mother's voice can be calming and can help build a natural and physiological bond with your sons. It is imperative that your unborn sons are surrounded by a warm and calming environment.

Chapter 3

The Benefits of Breastfeeding Your Baby

Breastfeeding is a process where a woman feeds her baby directly with milk from her breast or from a breast pump. Breastfeeding is the most naturally-occurring thing that can happen during childbirth.[2] The size of a woman's breast does not have any impact on whether she will be able to successfully breastfeed her baby.[2] Before a baby is born, prolactin is produced by the pituitary gland.[2] Oxytocin, also produced by the pituitary gland, is a hormone that stimulates the breast to eject milk.[2] While a woman is breastfeeding her baby, antioxidants are released in her milk. These antigens help to keep a baby's immune system strong. Human milk contains all the health ingredients that a baby needs. Some of the healthy ingredients contained in breast milk include protein, sugar, fat, and antibodies. Prolactin is a hormone that is widely known to relax a woman and make her feel happy and joyful. Oxytocin is widely known to cause strong feelings of love between you and your baby and is released during breastfeeding. Breastfeeding produces an emotional satisfaction between a mother and her baby. Babies that are not breastfed get sick more often than those that are breastfed. Babies that are not breastfed usually catch colds quicker and sometimes get more ear infections.[2] Breastfeeding a baby also decreases their risk of Sudden Infant Death Syndrome (SIDS).[1] Breastfeeding may seem intimidating, but women can talk to their doctors about their reservations. Find support groups that are available in your area to help you successfully breastfeed your sons. Breastfeeding is an extremely pleasant experience if your husband/partner/friend is supportive of you breastfeeding your babies. His decision to support you may heavily influence whether you breastfeed your sons or not. Talk to him about the benefits of breastfeeding. According to the American Academy of Pediatrics and the World Health Organization, they recommend that a woman breastfeed her baby for a minimum of six months and to continue with breastfeeding for a year after solid foods are introduced to the baby.[2] There are psychological benefits to breastfeeding your baby, too.[2] The closeness that the mom and baby experience is priceless. There is a physical connection that you two will hopefully share for the rest of your lives.

Every mother should consult with their doctors before deciding whether to breastfeed their baby. There are some instances when a mother should not breastfeed their baby due to a medical condition.[2] Before a woman has a baby, it would be an excellent idea to attend a breastfeeding class so that they learn as much as they can about the issue. Hospitals have lactation specialists, nurses, pediatricians, family doctors, and breastfeeding support groups to help a mother get started with breastfeeding her babies. It has been well-documented that breastfeeding may increase cognitive development in a child.[1] Hopefully, all soon-to-be moms will consider breastfeeding their babies. When a woman decides to breastfeed her baby, it takes planning ahead whenever she decides to go out with her baby.

A breastfeeding support system is available to all mothers for several months after they have a baby. The support system may include other women that are currently breastfeeding or used to breastfeed or the lactation specialist at the hospital. Every woman should consider the benefits of breastfeeding even if she was not a breastfed baby. Mothers should try to maintain a healthy diet while breastfeeding.

Another advantage to breastfeeding is healthy eating will always benefit your babies. Once a woman starts eating healthy to breastfeed her baby, her good eating habits may continue throughout her life. It is more acceptable now to breastfeed in public than it was in past years.[2] So, a woman should not feel embarrassed if other people are around while she wants to breastfeed her son. A breast milk pump is available for women to use when they are resting from their baby or they need to return to work. When a mother returns to work she may want to think about continuing to breastfeed. A lot of employers have lactation rooms available for breastfeeding moms. This would allow a mother to breastfeed her baby even longer. I was fortunate enough to be aware of the health benefits of breastfeeding a baby before my son was born so it is very important that I share this information with as many mothers as possible.

As soon as my son was born, he and I started off with a very strong emotional and physical bond. He happened to be one of those babies that naturally took to breastfeeding. I could tell that he enjoyed it based on the relaxed and calm look on his face whenever he was breastfeeding. Words cannot describe what it felt like. It was breathtaking whenever I watched my son look up into my eyes from time to time while he was breastfeeding. I oftentimes tell my son that one of the reasons to this day that we are so close is because I breastfed him. I feel such pride and joy from knowing that I took the time and effort to do this with him. I always wanted him to feel secure and trust that I would always be there for him, no matter what. I also breastfed my son because I knew that breastfeeding him would contribute toward increasing his cognitive development. I absolutely loved breastfeeding my son knowing that it was the best thing for him. I also believe it is one of the reasons that he is so intelligent. I oftentimes breastfed my son in the back seat of my truck whenever I was in public or the women's lounge inside an extremely clean bathroom at the mall. If I was over a friend's house, then it was never a problem with breastfeeding him in another room. Before I had my son, I bought two breastfeeding cushions. I left one inside my house and I put the other one in the back of my truck. I did not want to have to remember to carry it along every time I left my house. I also carried a blanket so that I could cover up if I needed to breastfeed in public. Since I stayed at home and breastfed my son for so long he did not start going to a day care facility until he was almost two years old. I know that every mom cannot afford to stay at home for a lengthy time, but if you can it is worth breastfeeding your baby and waiting until your child is older before they start going to a day care facility. So, when my doctor asked me if I was planning on breastfeeding my son, it was an instantaneous "yes."

Chapter 4

Cultivate Your Sons Into Enthusiastic Readers

Reading books will open-up the world to your sons. Start reading to your sons when they are inside your womb. It will allow them to explore and wonder about their surroundings and will also expand their curiosity once they are born. Even if you do not enjoy reading, your sons will love that you took time to read to them. This is especially important when your sons are preschool age so that they begin forming and learning new words. Reading is a way to boost your sons educational knowledge as they get older. In this society, most of your sons are being raised in an environment where they need to answer more than just yes and no questions. They need to learn to answer questions that require them to have a conversation with their parents or other individuals that are talking to them.

My son reads a lot of books. It is amazing that I never had to force him to read at an early age. Before he could read, I always read to him every day. When he was younger, my daily routine was to bathe him, rub his body, and then read to him before he went to bed. At night, whenever I finished reading to him I would always cut out the bedroom light and leave his bedroom. Whenever he woke up at night I would turn on the light in his bedroom and then read to him until he fell back asleep or sing to him. If that did not work, then I would turn on quiet classical music on his radio. As my son grew older and became an adolescent, I always made him take more time to read books. One way to do this was to limit his playing video games and to have him to take along a book in the car as we rode out for appointments or to run errands.

Chapter 5

Shape Your Sons Mindset

I constantly speak to my son about his mindset. Why are so many boys satisfied with being an average student but there are also boys that are not satisfied with being an average student? Oftentimes it depends on what the boys think about themselves. If your sons think that they are smart, then they are smart. If your sons want to be an Honor Roll student, then he must think that he is an Honor Roll student. Why is it that the same two students receive the same information in a classroom and one of the students does extremely well and the other student does not do well? It is the mindset of both students. One of the students thinks that they will do well and the other thinks that they will not do well. It is important that your sons are "hungry" to do well. Some students are "hungry" to do well in school but being "hungry" can apply to their life as well. It can apply to anything that your sons want to do in life. Your sons must keep telling themselves that they will do well at something and believing it so much that they do well. Your sons need good role models around them so that they can emulate them. The role model does not always have to be their mother or father. The role model can be an aunt or uncle or somebody else like a teacher or coach that is raising them.

It is always important for your sons to think positive thoughts and know that they can do anything in life that they want. The more that your sons think about themselves in a positive light the more that good things will happen to them. Have you ever had a friend or family member that always speaks negatively? You know that whenever this person does this that negative things usually happen to them. Whenever your sons think positive, they will exude more self-confidence toward other people. Also, positive things will usually happen to them. If your sons speak about negative things, then negative things will happen to them. I am such a strong believer about this. It does not mean that everything positive will happen in your sons lives. It means that the negative things will be hopefully kept to a minimum.

My son was raised to be a mentally-strong young man. All things are possible with God who strengthens me (Philippians 4:13) is a Bible verse that my son recites every day. I also told my son to say, "Positive Affirmations" about himself every day since he started being able to talk. I had him write "Positive Affirmations" on index cards that he believed about himself and post them on a vision board where he could see them every day and repeat them out loud. My son's index cards on his vision board say: 1) I will always strive for excellence, 2) I am a newspaper and television star, 3) I am a brilliant scholar, 4) I can do anything I want to do, 5) I will never quit, 6) I am a natural born leader, 7) I am a phenomenal athlete, 8) I am a National Junior Honor Society President and member, 9) I am a 5-time USA Track National Junior Olympian, 10) I am a 1-time Amateur Athletic Union Track National Junior Olympian, 11) I am a 2-time Amateur Athletic Union Track Regional Junior Olympian, 12) I will always think before I act, 13) I am handsome, 14) I am "The Man", and 15) Attract what you expect, reflect what you desire, become what you respect, and mirror what you admire. I decided to load up his vision board with "Positive Affirmations" that he could look at every day to remind and train his mind to think positive thoughts every day. I also hung a collage of pictures on the vision board. For each school year, I put up a picture of my son. I also put up pictures of my son when he won his first gold medal at the USA

Track and Field National Junior Olympics at Wichita State University when he was six years old and other national track medals as well. My son's "Positive Affirmations" index cards and pictures of himself accomplishing his athletic and academic goals bring a smile on his face every day.

Parents, discuss with your sons "Positive Affirmations" and how important it is for them to speak positive words that they believe about themselves to themselves and out loud too. Help them to come up with their own "Positive Affirmations" for themselves and post them somewhere in the house on a vision board where they can see and repeat them every day. It is very important that your sons arm themselves with a self-confidence armor before they leave the house every day.

My son has always wanted to excel as a student scholar. In the seventh and eighth grade, he applied and was awarded academic scholarships. When my son was in the seventh grade he was nominated and then inducted into the National Junior Honor Society (NJHS) at his private middle school. When he was in the eighth grade he was elected President of the NJHS. The NJHS is an organization in middle school that students are nominated and accepted into based on their scholarship, leadership, service, character, and citizenship. Being elected into NJHS is one of my son's highest academic accomplishments so far. My son earned a 4.17 Grade Point Average (GPA) in the seventh grade. In the seventh grade, he earned the highest GPA in the seventh grade Bible classes, the highest GPA in the Science, Technology, Engineering, and Math, (STEM) classes, and the Math Club Outstanding Service as a Student Teacher award. In the first semester of eighth grade, my son earned a 5.0 GPA. My son did not make it to this point in his life overnight. It took years of vigorous work and sacrifice that is paying off in his life and will in your sons' lives as well. Due to my son's excellent academic record, he will attend a very prestigious Catholic high school as an Honors student. My son was groomed for countless hours to prepare academically for this opportunity.

CHAPTER 6

DEVELOP ECONOMIC REASONING IN YOUR SONS

Teach Your Sons About Money

Constantly teach your sons about the value of money. Arm your sons with the necessary financial tools for them to be successful in life. It is imperative that you teach your sons how to make money and budget their money for their financial life. It is important that your sons become financially stable so that they can provide for themselves later in their lives. These skills are needed to build financial wealth and freedom and allow your sons to live their dreams. Set up a college savings plan when they are young. Take your sons with you to the bank to open an account in their name. Whenever you conduct transactions with their savings, checking, and money market accounts they should be at the bank with you as much as possible.

CHAPTER 7

PATHWAYS TO BUILD SELF-CONFIDENCE IN YOUR SONS

It is very important that you know what your sons think of themselves. It gives you a measuring stick to gauge whether you need to work more with them to build their self-confidence or whether they are on the right track to being self-confident. Self-confidence is built on your son's successes in life. Yours sons should learn from their failures too. Teach them not to be afraid to fail. So many individuals are afraid of failure and never risk learning or growing more because fear holds them back. Even when your sons lose, they win because of all the lessons that they learn from losing because with failure people do not try. Failure should be a great motivator to your sons to improve themselves. If your sons try something once or twice and fail, then they should want to try again. When your sons have a strategy that aligns with a purpose, things will happen. Things will happen even if your sons do not want them to. Tell your sons all the time to keep living their purpose in life with a strategy in mind. There will be moments when things will not go right and moments when everything goes right for them. Great parents know this so teach your sons this so that they can survive when things do not go their way.

I will never forget when my son was in kindergarten he earned a NS, Not Satisfactory, in his handwriting class in the first quarter. He was five years old at the time and we talked with him about him needing to improve his handwriting skills. We told him that we would team up with his kindergarten teacher to make this happen. It was amazing that he wanted to improve his handwriting and there was no resistance at all on his part. It also helped that my son genuinely liked his kindergarten teacher. The second quarter he earned a Satisfactory grade, the third quarter he earned a Good grade, and then in the fourth quarter he earned an Outstanding grade. This was one of my son's first educational lessons that whenever he worked hard at his school work that he would do well.

Encourage Your Sons To Be Assertive

As parents, you do not ever want your sons to suppress or hide their feelings from you. Also, parents should not want their sons to be afraid of their reactions whenever they do something wrong. Your sons will gradually learn to have a balance between expressing certain feelings and controlling other feelings. This comes with maturity so, until then, be patient with them. Encourage your sons to ask for what they want in life. If they do not, then they will never get whatever it is they want in life. Some current school systems are instilling passive characteristics into young boys. The school systems do not want boys to act assertive. This is why it is so important at home to reinforce to your sons that it is perfectly okay for your sons to be assertive at school and other places as well. It is disheartening to watch some of our young boys not being groomed to be extraordinary young men and leaders. Instead, a lot of them are being groomed to be followers and not great leaders, not developing their full potential because they have not been pushed by their parents or the school systems to be assertive. Teachers sometime email parents about the most minor issues. It almost seems as though they want the boys to behave perfectly. No young boy is always going to behave perfectly. It seems that there is no system in place that allows boys to make mistakes and not be perfect. As a result, some young boys are becoming less and less assertive. They are not taught to fight back in certain situations or stick up for themselves. And if they do fight back they always get into trouble and are chastised for doing so. This can sometimes lead to them always feeling bad about the way that they handled a situation. This is not necessary. As a society, we need to learn how to better teach young boys that it is okay to make mistakes. At home, parents should take the time to instill in their sons that it is okay to make mistakes and they do not have to act like robots.

Encourage Independent and Inquisitive Thinkers

Let your sons know that it is okay to think outside the box. Parents need to raise more sons in our society who are not ordinary thinkers, but extraordinary thinkers. More extraordinary thinkers are needed that are creative and not afraid to take risks in business, science or any field they choose to pursue. As great parents you should want to raise inquisitive sons. Whoever your sons associate with should be just as smart as your own sons so that they can learn from them as well. Great minds think alike. My son is an extraordinary thinker. He has always asked a lot of questions. Once you answer one of his questions, the answers will lead him to ask more questions. My son never takes anything that you say at face value but always wants to go into more depth to understand an issue more.

<u>Do Not Force Your Sons To Change</u>

One of the best things that parents can do for their sons is to try and let them naturally develop into their own beings. Gently guide them into their next stage of life so that they can become young men of good character. If your sons are having difficulty adjusting to a different stage in their lives, try and be as patient as you can with them. Give them the room to make errors. It may take your sons a little while to adjust to the change.

CHAPTER 8

INTRODUCE YOUR SONS TO HEALTHY FOODS

Do not allow your sons to eat a lot of sweets or candy. They should eat plenty of vegetables and fruit. Allow your sons to experience grocery shopping with you and try to make it fun for them. It is critical that your son's practice having healthy eating habits to prevent diseases such as obesity later in life. A stronger effort is needed from schools, teachers, counselors, and parents to monitor young boys eating habits and educate them about diseases such as obesity that may affect them now or in the future. Parents, talk with your son's teachers at schools and ask them to assign research projects on the long-term impact of obesity on heart disease, high blood pressure, and stroke and to discuss healthy eating habits with the students. Your sons could research obesity and offer suggestions on how to better address this issue. Parents can informally monitor their son's eating habits at school and at home. Make sure that your sons are drinking and eating healthy snacks like peanuts, almonds, dried fruits, juice, and sports drinks instead of eating a lot of candy and drinking a lot of sodas. Make sure that the menus that are offered at your son's schools provide more nutritious options for them such as salad bars and baked foods rather than French fries, hamburgers, pizza, and other fatty and greasy foods. The school systems should consult with dietitians and nutritionists on selecting healthy menus.

A Poster Session on Obesity can be a suggested program at your son's school. Awards could be given for the best poster that would be judged on content, presentation, and comprehensiveness for first, second, and third place. Public health professionals and various community members from the local areas could serve as judges. The participation by these individuals conveys a passionate sense of community support and interest in the students' education and well-being. An Obesity Awareness Day could be held each year at your son's school. Public health professionals could be invited to participate and lecture on issues related to obesity. Private representatives could also be invited to staff booths and informally talk with students about the issue. Brochures and pamphlets could be distributed to the students that discusses obesity.

If your sons are exposed to healthier foods in their school environment, then they may become more passionate about eating healthy and change their eating habits. The Poster Session on Obesity and an Obesity Awareness Day and other health issues could then be duplicated at the regional and state levels.

CHAPTER 9

SPEND QUALITY TIME WITH YOUR SONS

Pick a special time each day to pray together as a family and worship together, too. Praying will show your sons that they should never be too busy to spend quality time with God. This will help them to build their own relationship with God and reinforce Christian characteristics such as compassion, courage, self-control, love of others, faith, perseverance, godliness, and brotherly kindness. Your relationship with your sons will also be stronger. Pray about various topics affecting your family.

Teach your son's life skills such as cooking so that they will learn to be independent and be able to take care of themselves. Your sons should know how to clean, wash clothes, and wash dishes. Always make time to talk, play board games, listen, and constantly interact with your sons.

Your son's homework and class work should be reviewed on a regular schedule. Spend some extra time practicing school work with them so that they will do well. Praise your sons for the school work that they have done well, and explanations should be given about why they got an answer wrong. Parents should be patient enough to explain concepts to your sons again and again if they do not understand it the first time. Hopefully they will ask questions if they do not understand a topic.

Videotape your sons whenever they participate in school activities, sports, church activities, and day care center activities. Download the videotapes to CDs or to the computer for their enjoyment as they get older. Keep a scrapbook for your sons that allows them to see pictures of themselves, book reports, letters, special art projects that they made in school, camp, and other places. Write letters to your sons on special holidays (Easter, Mother's Day, Father's Day, Hanukkah, Christmas, Kwanzaa, Thanksgiving) and other special occasions like birthdays and graduations throughout the year and describe their special accomplishments and goals that they have set and met for themselves. Consider laminating their letters and other special items such as sports certificates, honor roll certificates, and other important certificates and put them in a portfolio for them to cherish later in their life.

Always be encouraging and motivating to your sons with positive words so that your sons know how proud their parents are of them; do not let them ever take for granted that they know that you are proud of them. Try to limit the amount of time that you talk on your cell phone or home telephone, unless it is an emergency, while you are talking, playing at the park, or spending quality time with your sons. Many parents seem to make the mistake of incessantly talking on their cell phones while they are in grocery stores, at the mall, at the park, and other places which takes time away from your sons. Tell your sons as often as you can how you feel about them and how much you love them. It will help to build their self-confidence. Always send messages to your sons that they are valuable to you and are always worth your time. Whenever you spend time with your sons, be sure to keep your focus directly on them and not anywhere else. Spending quality time with your sons is important. The more time that you spend with your sons when they are young will establish the more time that they will want to spend with you as you get older.

It is extremely important to take quality time to talk with your sons to answer questions that they have about their lives. Taking time to talk with them as they get older is even more important. Especially when your sons begin adolescence. A parent can never turn the clock back in time and wish that they had spent more time with their son if they did not when they were growing up. So, the lesson learned is to not take time for granted and spend as much time with your sons whenever you can. Life is too short. I know of a lot of women that put more time into their careers than their sons. Some women can balance their careers and motherhood well, but others are not as successful at it. Unfortunately, some of these women that are not able to balance motherhood and their careers well may realize later in their sons' lives that they should have spent more time with them when they were younger. Sometimes this is because these women did not have the necessary time to spend with their sons because their jobs were so demanding. Also, these same women are a lot more stressed out from their busy jobs, which causes them to have less patience and love to show toward their sons. This can lead to their sons possibly becoming withdrawn from them and feeling depressed. If you notice any serious behavioral changes or signs of depression in your sons, then make sure that you get the necessary help for them.

CHAPTER 10

FOSTER OPEN COMMUNICATION WITH YOUR SONS

After picking up your sons from school, ask them how their day was. What happened? What did they have fun doing for the day? What did they not enjoy doing for the day? Ask if there is anything they want to share with you. Always take time to listen to your sons. Allow them to talk about any subject with you. When they know that you are truly listening to them it will validate their feelings. Hopefully they will then be open with you about comfortable as well as uncomfortable topics. You should always want your sons to feel comfortable enough to talk with you about any subject. They will hopefully want to confide in you and not keep any secrets from you.

When your sons turn around twelve or thirteen years old their doctor will normally ask you to step out of the room during physical examinations. I had no problem with this when the time came. I am sure that a lot of parents may be uncomfortable with stepping out of the room, but the doctors want your sons to have an open dialogue with them because they want your sons to trust them. They want your sons to feel comfortable enough to ask them questions if they do not want to ask their parents about or discuss certain issues with them. Parents should also want their sons to have open communication with their doctors in addition to themselves.

CHAPTER 11

FAMILY INTERACTION TIPS AND GUIDELINES

<u>Parents Should Be Teammates</u>

It is extremely important that parents work together to raise their sons. One voice should be heard by your sons to prevent unnecessary confusion among them. Your sons need to see that both of you have a good relationship with each other by being loving and respectful toward each other. Oftentimes, your sons will naturally emulate what they see from their parents and other adults that they trust. Parents should split household duties between themselves and then alternate checking homework with your sons. Mothers, it is important that you leave your "power heels" at the front door when you get home after work every day and become Mommy to your sons. It is okay to be a powerful career woman but be careful about wanting to control everything at home and not compromise with some issues.

"Me Time"

Parents should take time away from taking care of your sons throughout the year. Everybody deserves to take a break from parenting. Being a good parent takes a lot of time and effort. A break will give parents time to recuperate and recharge your energy level. The break can be for a short or long time. Hire a babysitter or ask your family or friends to take care of your sons while you spend time with yourselves, others, or doing something else that you enjoy. You will feel so refreshed when you do this, and it will allow you to be extremely patient with your sons.

Discipline Your Sons

Discipline is needed in all homes. Your sons may not know the importance of being disciplined but your sons need discipline in their lives. I have talked with a lot of coaches and teachers that tell me that the boys that come from homes that have more discipline are the boys that are better able to focus in school and accomplish goals they set for themselves. Discipline gives boys structure and organization that makes a difference about how they respond to things in their own lives. There are always opportunities for parents to use discipline as teaching moments for your sons to set them on the right path in life. These moments will stick with your sons throughout their lives.

Whenever I discipline my son, I try to spend a lot of time explaining things to him. I want him to know why I am disciplining him. I do this as much as I can instead of yelling at him about everything. Doing this allows me to help him to understand his thinking process instead of him focusing on how angry I am. Although I am extremely angry many times, it is more important for him to understand why I am angry and what he can do the next time when he is faced with the same kind of situation. It is imperative that you let your sons know that everybody has made mistakes in their lives. It is not how many mistakes you make that is most important but that you learn from those mistakes. Nobody is perfect and no one in this world is immune from making mistakes. I always tell my son that it is okay to make mistakes in life but that you must always learn from the situation and try not to make the same mistake again. Sometimes your sons will make the same mistakes, but they should keep trying anyway.

Offer Incentives To Your Sons

Reward your sons with incentives when they do well in school, sports, and other activities. The incentives do not have to be expensive. They can be small tokens such as video games, gum, lollipops, money, books, or restaurant meals. Incentives such as these will give your sons something to look forward to when they do well. Rewarding your sons can also help them to feel a sense of accomplishment. This will also help build their self-confidence and self-esteem. Incentives will help them work hard at whatever they are doing. Also, your sons may challenge and push themselves to do even better the next time at something.

Chapter 12

Keep Your Sons Safe

Always make sure that you know your son's whereabouts. They do not necessarily have to be right next to you, but you should at least know their whereabouts and what time they plan to return home. Parents, it does not take a long time to lose sight of your sons, especially if your sons have enough time when you turn your back and they can walk away. Since parents know that this can happen, it is imperative that they keep as close a watch on their sons as possible. Do not let your sons go to a public restroom by themselves until they are a certain age to be able to handle themselves in a dangerous situation. Once they start going to the bathroom by themselves, parents should still stand outside the bathroom door for safety reasons. Anything could happen to your sons in the bathroom if an insane adult or older child has enough time to harm them. Also, be careful about leaving your sons alone with an adult that you do not trust. Be careful with whom you let spend time around your sons. Your sons should usually be around other boys that are about the same age as them. For the most part your sons should not be allowed around boys that are much older than them. This can be unsafe. There are some exceptions to this of course. Never ever put your sons in a situation that could potentially lead to them being harmed or molested. Do not allow your sons to go over any other boys' houses that you do not personally know. Going to the basketball courts, playgrounds, and other places should be off limits with other boys whom you have never even met before. Invite your sons' friends over to your house or set up play dates with them. This gives parents a chance to observe their son's social style. Parents will be able to intervene with discipline when needed, individually or as a group. Peer pressure will usually begin to become a major factor in your sons' lives around seven or eight years old. So, your sons must be self-confident and comfortable when interacting with other boys by this time, if not earlier.

Bullying and Self-Defense

Bullying has been occurring more and more to young boys as time goes by. More measures need to be put in place so that your sons will not be afraid of other boys.

Your sons should be taught how to defend themselves. Unfortunately, in this day and time, at least once in their lives your sons will probably be teased by another boy. Regardless of where you choose to raise your sons this will happen. Boys can be very mean and cruel to each other. Some of the boys that are doing the bullying may be raised in homes where they are not taught about the importance of not being cruel to others.

CHAPTER 13

CONTROL YOUR SONS ELECTRONIC USE

Electronics Are Bad Influences

Allowing your sons to spend an enormous amount of time indoors will cripple their minds. Since computers have taken over the world, a lot of boys are spending a lot of time indoors playing video games, watching television and videos, and playing computer games. However, it is important for your sons to get exercise outdoors, too. They need at least twenty to thirty minutes of exercise a day. Exercising is good for your sons' cardiovascular system and to develop their brains.

There is entirely too much nudity on television and videos and too much profanity in songs that are on the radio or on videos or on television. Parents should monitor what their sons are watching and listening to on the radio. If parents do not do this, then you will see your sons imitating what they see and hear on the television and on the radio. Some of the behavior that your sons will see and hear is not appropriate for them and may have a negative influence on them. Most of the time the women that are in the videos on television or on the computer are not appropriately dressed and are not portraying themselves as self-confident women. These videos that your sons may see and hear can have a bad influence on their mind.

It is okay for your sons to love playing video games if they do not let the games control their every waking moment and thoughts. I suggest that parents have a time limit for allowing their sons to play video games. I know how much fun video games are, but video games can also be very addictive. They may interfere with your son's ability to get their school work completed and may affect their grades. Especially during the week when your sons need to fully concentrate on their school work. No good can come from being addicted to video games. We have rules in our house about video games. On weekdays (Monday through Thursday), my son has a time limit for playing video games. He cannot get on video games until he is finished with his homework. Once he is finished with his homework, he is only allowed to play video games for one hour. On weekends (Friday, Saturday, and Sunday), he can play video games for four hours or so each day. If I notice a drop in any of his grades, then my son knows that he can no longer be on video games on the weekdays or the weekends until his grades improve.

Cell Phones Tempt Teens To Text Late At Night

Seriously consider having your sons, especially when they are teenagers, to turn their cell phones off at night and to give them to you at a certain time. The times may vary each day depending on whether it is a school night or the weekend. You may want to allow them to talk and text more on the weekends or holidays. Taking away their cell phones at night will allow them to not be tempted to text or talk on their cell phones throughout the night. Cell phones can be very distracting to your sons and they may interfere with the amount of time that they rest at night. Your sons need to get a certain amount of rest each night to do well in school the next day.

CHAPTER 14

HELP YOUR SONS ACHIEVE ACADEMIC EXCELLENCE

Instill A Love Of Learning

Try to make learning fun and engaging so that your sons will want to learn at school. Almost weekly, when my son was young, we would visit a local Science Center. Although it was rather costly to pay each time, I ended up purchasing an annual membership because we visited so often. An annual membership was more cost effective than paying each time we visited. He absolutely loved every time we went to the Science Center. The Science Center had a Kids Room where my son had hands-on exposure and it was fascinating. They even had animals that he watched and touched. We also visited museums and other educational places as well.

Parents should encourage their sons to want to learn about various subject areas when they are very young. Your sons will always feed off the energy of their parents. If you display excitement about learning different subject areas that your sons are learning in school, then they will be excited to learn about them too. If parents show boredom, then your sons will be bored as well and will not show enthusiasm to learn anything new.

Build Leadership Skills

Certain leadership skills are innate but other traits can be learned. You should put your sons in environments where they can learn to lead. One of the greatest characteristics of being a great leader is if they can inspire others to be their greatest and to dream big. Raise your sons in a way so that they can be an inspiration to other boys. This is especially true of my son. He is such an inspiration to other boys and girls as well.

Connect With Your Sons' Teachers

Volunteer to be a chaperone and attend as many activities as possible with your sons. This allows your sons to learn about the world and cultural surroundings. Families that are involved in their children's education usually results in students that do better in school. It is important that parents evaluate their son's school every year to ensure that they are receiving a quality education. Observe your sons' teachers, classmates, and surroundings, and you can learn what needs to be supplemented or what needs to be reinforced at your home. Stay in close contact with your son's teachers throughout the year to monitor their progress in school. Periodically email and schedule parent-teacher conferences with your son's teachers to find out the progress that your sons are making in each of their subject areas. It is very important that parents have a good relationship with your sons' teachers. At no time should you be trying to tell them how to teach in their classrooms, but you should always work with their teachers so that your sons can continue to do better in school. Whenever your sons are having trouble in a subject area then you should ask their teachers to suggest books, readings, or internet sites so that you can help your sons understand the information. If this does not help, then you should consider hiring a tutor for your sons.

I have never sensed that contacting a teacher to try and help my son improve his grade was a problem. Even if it was a problem, it is important to prepare my son for the next level of school. This is not just for now but also for later in my son's life. One reason that it has never been a problem has been my approach to the situation. I work directly with the teacher and figure out whether my son needs to change his approach or study strategy at home or improve a study skill. The relationship between a teacher and a parent should be a partnership.

Any prospective schools that your sons may attend should be carefully considered. If money allows you to enroll your sons in private or religious schools, that is great. These schools will keep their minds focused more than public schools and they will learn certain disciplines and practices that they will not learn if they are enrolled in public schools. Private school students are assigned homework that is more challenging to complete than public school students. Private school curriculums are more challenging and will better prepare your sons academically for college than public school curriculums.

Attend High School Open Houses

It is a great idea to attend high school open houses two to three years before your son enters the ninth grade. This will give him the opportunity to meet potential teachers and other staff at a prospective high school. Ask questions about their teaching styles and about their curriculum. Take your sons along to the open houses so that they can tour the school and ask any questions that they want as well. Another way to expose your sons to a potential high school is by enrolling them in summer camps and other programs that are held for youth at the school. This was one of the ways that my son met different teachers and coaches at the high school he will attend. It is never too early to start exposing your sons to the next level of school. My son started going to potential high schools' open houses when he was in the sixth grade. He thoroughly enjoyed the visits and he asked a lot of questions. He asked good questions to the teachers and coaches that I might not have asked myself. It truly was a positive experience for my son.

Tour Colleges And Universities With Your Sons

Visit as many colleges and universities as you can with your sons. My son was exposed to several colleges and universities from the time that he was young. When he was six years old, we travelled with him to Wichita State University in Wichita, Kansas for him to compete in the USA Track and Field National Junior Olympics in the 4 x 100 relay in front of thousands of people.

For several years, my son participated in several high school and college football and basketball camps where he had the chance to meet and talk with several college and National Football League and National Basketball Association players. By the end of the camps, several of the players would always notice my son's speed, quickness, and agility. Several of them would always tell him that he had good foot work which is essential for any boy that wants to be a good football or basketball player. My son would tell the players that he runs track and they would always ask him what events he ran. These are priceless conversations and experiences that not only built my son's character but also his self-confidence.

Push/Pressure Your Sons Academically

Not enough boys are being pushed by their parents to achieve academic excellence. Whenever I interact with a lot of parents, I notice that they are babying their sons and making things as easy as possible for them and not pushing them to achieve academic excellence. So many of these parents allow their sons to constantly complain to them, even about the tiniest things. Whatever happened to letting boys know that they must work hard academically and in life to achieve whatever dreams and goals they have set for themselves and have them reinforce this with their actions? Whenever your sons start complaining about something, you need to sternly remind them about working hard in school and in life as often as possible. This is a must so that they know that everything in their life, including academics, will not go their way or as they plan. Your sons must be able to deal with disappointment, like low grades, and be able to rebound from it. The earlier that they learn this, the better able they will be to deal with these and other issues as well.

Your sons will achieve academic excellence if they establish a daily study routine. If you start a routine when your sons are young they will always know what time to do their homework. Being able to focus should naturally become a part of your sons because it was a learned behavior for them. I started a routine with my son when he was young. He continued to follow it and stays focused with completing his school work. His routine has always been that whenever he gets home from school he takes a short break to get a snack and relax for about thirty minutes and then immediately starts his homework. As my son became older he got to the point where he began to become more and more aware of when it was time for him to complete his homework, shower, eat his dinner, and go to bed.

I always prepared my son for the next level of school or the next grade. When he was a toddler, I started preparing him for kindergarten. When he was in the fourth grade, I started preparing him for middle school. I made sure that I attended the middle school open house and I also started to get to know the middle school principal and guidance counselor. When he was in middle school, I started preparing him for high school. I worked with my son to become more and more responsible and independent and how to keep himself as organized as possible with his school work. My son's routine was established early, so he was always able to maintain good grades. Now keep in mind that when your son is transitioning from elementary school to middle school, or middle school to high school, you will need to allow an adjustment period for your sons. It may be a few weeks, or it may be an entire quarter or semester for them to adjust to their new routine. Either way, try and be as patient as possible with your son. My son, who has always been on Honor Roll, Distinguished Honor Roll, or Chancellors Honor Roll, needed a few weeks to adjust to middle school. Ever since my son was in kindergarten, I always reached out well before Progress Report time to a teacher. I never waited until Progress Report time if I noticed any low grades. In my son's case, any grade that is lower than an A is a low grade for him. I watch his grades and whenever they are lower than an A, I would get in touch with the teacher to find out how my son could improve his grade.

Academic Extracurricular Activities Are Essential

Take as much time as possible to have your sons participate in academic extracurricular activities. It will give your sons a chance to learn outside the classroom in a fun environment. It is widely known that academic extracurricular activities can be a positive influence on your sons.[3,4] Search around your local area for activities that may interest your sons. Your local YMCA, county recreation centers, and local colleges and universities probably have something of interest to you and your sons. A few suggestions are Science, Technology, Engineering, and Math (STEM) and Science, Technology, Engineering, Art, and Math (STEAM) Programs, Art Clubs, Math Clubs, Science Clubs, Language Clubs, Writing Clubs, and many other programs like these. The clubs can reinforce the subject material that your sons are currently learning, recently learned, or learning in the future. It would be ideal if the program is sponsored by a local college or university. This would allow your sons to be exposed to a college atmosphere at an early age.

CHAPTER 15

ESTABLISH ATHLETIC GOALS WITH YOUR SONS

Involve Your Sons In Sports

Sometimes, parents do not want their sons to participate in sports. There is an impression that they will get hurt playing certain sports. Allow your sons to participate in sports. Participating in sports builds teamwork, independence, self-confidence, the desire not to give up, and the desire to be successful. It will also allow your sons to work well together with other boys, set priorities, and celebrate team accomplishments. If you want your sons to develop a natural interest in sports then attend sporting events such as basketball, football, soccer, and baseball games with them. If you enroll your son's in sports, then do not just drop them off for practices. Stay and talk with the coach after practices, watch your sons practices and give them additional one-on-one pointers, especially if you are a former athlete.

If you want your sons to grow up to be mentally-strong young men, then you must stop coddling them and allow them to participate in sports. If your sons participate in sports it will teach them that when they experience tough times to pick themselves up and keep going. Most of the time, mothers play a key role in whether their sons participate in sports. If mothers do not want their sons to participate in sports, then they usually do not. Fathers, whenever this happens you need to talk with your wife or partner and let her know the importance of your sons being able to participate in sports. Individual training and coaching for your sons may be good for them. It may be good for them to be a part of a sports team, but sometimes individual attention may be better for them. It will give your sons a chance to ask questions and get individual attention. Consider coaching one of your sons' sports teams. It will give you a chance to not only spend quality time with your sons but for them to get hands-on teaching from you.

<u>Stop Over-Pressuring Your Sons
To Get Athletic Scholarships</u>

I talk to parents all the time who are consumed with pushing their young sons too hard for them to get athletic scholarships to college. It is one thing to push and motivate your sons to do their best. It is another thing to push your sons into trying to get athletic college scholarships at an early age. Especially if you are trying to live through your sons and have them accomplish something in their lives that you did not. Your sons excelling in academics must be just as important to you as them excelling in sports. I talk with a lot of parents whose sons are good in sports but do not have good grades. In addition, these boys have a challenging time getting a high SAT score so that they can get into a college. What a total shame this is when it happens. Most of the time I blame the parents for not stressing the importance of education enough to their sons at an early age. If parents did, then more boys would know the importance of education and would apply, be accepted, and go to college.

Parents should not bank on their sons getting an athletic scholarship to college. They should not be over-bearing toward their sons about it, either. Parents should have their sons participate in sports for the right reasons. Let your sons dream and make a path on their own and learn to also consider academic scholarships as well. Give your sons a chance to dream and follow their own path in life.

So many parents enroll their young sons in a sports program or team and never meet the coach or attend any of their games. That is plain selfish. Your sons always need your support. You should want to know the adults that are spending time around your sons and what they are teaching them and how they are possibly influencing their thinking. Parents should want to know what type of person the coach is. Is the coach building your son's self-confidence up or tearing it apart? The only way that parents will know this is by getting to know the coach. This cannot happen if parents never meet the coach or spend time with them. I have talked with numerous coaches that are amazed at the number of parents that only drop-off and pick-up their sons from practice and that is the most interaction that they have with them. No parental involvement from them at all. Make sure that you are always supportive of your sons even if you did not grow up participating in sports. It is still very important for you to watch your sons' practices and games. A good youth coach will welcome parental involvement and support. Your parental involvement is another way to show that you care about your sons and whom they are around. This is especially important if your sons are young and impressionable.

Ever since my son was young, he was involved with several different sports teams. I have interacted and noticed several things about a lot of competitive parents. A lot of their sons are afraid to face their parents after they have not done well in a sport. Sometimes they delay having to go home so that they do not have to immediately see their parents. In some cases, their parents are mad when they have not done well. Some parents are just acting silly when they display negative energy like this toward their sons. Some of these parents are former athletes themselves and were good and have the same expectations for their sons. Some parents were not good in sports, so they put an enormous amount of pressure on their sons because they want them to be good. Are these parents displaying negative behavior like this because they want their sons to get an athletic scholarship to college? Whatever the reasons are, I hope that these parents will one day realize that they are damaging their sons' self-confidence every time they are displaying negative behavior like this toward them. These competitive parents may end up permanently damaging their sons' self-esteem and confidence. Hopefully they can start catching themselves before they get so angry in these situations. Parents need to realize that it is not that serious. Let your sons be themselves and stop putting so much pressure on them. Being good in sports should not be more important to parents than their sons growing up with self-confidence. I never enjoy interacting with parents that act like this. Every time I interact with a parent that displays negative behavior like this I try to politely point out to them that not every child is going to excel in sports. If your son does not excel in sports, then accept this and expose your sons to as many other activities as you can to determine which ones they are good at. It may be that your sons can participate in sports to build a healthy lifestyle that they can carry with them into adulthood. You as parents should want your sons to do well, but not at their own expense. My son is a phenomenal athlete, but we still never believed in putting pressure on him to excel in sports because we both realize that our son is his own individual and it is more important to show support toward him regardless of how well he does, not only in sports but with all other activities in his life as well.

<u>Overbearing Sports Parents</u>

If your sons are involved in sports, it is important that parents talk with the coach whenever their sons are not being motivated or uplifted, not just to complain.

If you feel that your sons are not doing well and could improve then there is no need to talk with the coach. Do not approach the coach with your sons based on your sons thinking that they are doing better than they did. This type of behavior sends a bad message to your sons. It shows your sons that you are willing to approach a coach even when your sons are not doing well athletically instead of talking with them about the importance of working harder to improve. Your sons are not always going to win in life, so they need to accept losing. I have talked with so many over-bearing parents it was unreal. I am amazed at how so many parents are so driven for their sons to do well in sports. Are these parents just as passionate about their sons doing well in school? I doubt it, because most of the time I never hear these parents talk about how well their sons are doing in school. They mostly talk about how good their sons are in sports.

Parents sacrifice a lot of their personal time if their sons participate in sports. They commit to taking their sons back and forth to practices as well as to games. Sometimes the games are held locally but they can also be held regionally, especially if your sons are on traveling sports teams. Some of the most demanding sports are track and swimming. Track and swim meets can last from early in the morning until very late in the afternoon and evening. So, if your sons participate in track or swimming it will require a lot more of your time than some of the other sports.

CHAPTER 16

LOOK AHEAD IN LIFE

Teach your sons to always look ahead in life by setting goals for themselves. If goals are not set for your sons, how will they know where they are trying to go in life? When my son was a baby I always bought toys, books, and other educational items that were a year or two, sometimes even three years older than he was at the time. I also bought age-appropriate toys for him, too, in addition to the challenging items. From an early age I taught my son to look ahead in life. When he was in elementary school we started thinking about where he would go to middle school. When my son was in middle school we started thinking about where he would go to high school. When he is in high school we will think about where he will go to college. When my son is in college, he will think about what he will do to get started with a job and how he will make it happen.

Notes

1. Breastfeeding and Breast Milk: Condition Information, US National Institutes of Health. Eunice Kennedy Shriver National Institute of Child Health and Human Development, US National Institutes of Health, http://www. nichd.nih.gov/health/topics/breastfeeding.

2. W.L. Stuhldreher, Ph.D., Breastfeeding, Salem Press Encyclopedia of Science, January 2017.

3. A. Holland, and T. Andre, Participation in extracurricular activities in secondary school: what is known, what needs to be known?, Review of Educational Research, 57, 437-466, 1987.

4. M.J. Harvancik and G. Golsan, Academic success and participation in high school and extracurricular activities: Is there a relationship?, American Psychological Association Meeting, Washington, D.C., August 1986.

Printed in the United States
By Bookmasters